LADYBUGS

Written By: Anna DiGilio

All rights reserved. No part of this publication may be reproduced, distributed, or transmitted in any form or by any means, including photocopying, recording, or other electronic or mechanical methods, without the prior written permission of the publisher, except in the case of brief quotations embodied in critical reviews and certain other noncommercial uses permitted by copyright law.

For permission requests, write to the publisher:
Laprea Publishing
info@lapreapublishing.com

Website: www.GuidedReaders.com

ISBN: 978-1-64579-584-1

© 2019 Anna DiGilio

Photo Credits:
Cover, Title Page: Depositphotos; Tihon6. 3: Depositphotos; Vladvitek. 4: Depositphotos; Taden1. 5: Depositphotos; Vencav. 6: Depositphotos; Fireflyphoto. 7 (top): Depositphotos; Ale-ks. 7 (bottom): Depositphotos; Georgios. 8 (top front): Depositphotos; Alexynder. 8 (top back): Depositphotos; TaiChesco. 8 (bottom): Depositphotos; Gvictoria. 9 (top): Depositphotos; Haveseen. 9 (bottom): Depositphotos; Koldunov. 10: Depositphotos; Nik_Merkulov. 11: Depositphotos; Dr.PAS. 12 (top, bottom): Depositphotos; Stroppy1. 13: Depositphotos; Vencav. 14 (top): Depositphotos; Manfredxy. 14 (bottom): Depositphotos; 719010835.qq.com.

TABLE OF CONTENTS

Features of Ladybugs .... Page 4

A Color of Defense .... Page 7

They Fly! .... Page 10

More Ladybugs .... Page 12

Ladybug Helpers .... Page 14

Glossary .... Page 15

Features of Ladybugs

Ladybugs are insects. They are red. Most have black dots. Many people think they're cute.

There are some <u>myths</u> about these bugs. They are not all girls! There are male ladybugs, too.

They do not all have spots. Some can have up to twenty spots! Some have none.

Many spots

No spots

A Color of Defense

Most ladybugs are red. Why? Red helps ladybugs. It's a defense. In nature, red is special. Red means "danger." Red might mean <u>poison</u>.

Some animals don't eat ladybugs. They fear getting sick.

Ladybugs also use smell for defense. They spray yellow fluid. It stinks! Predators stay away.

They Fly!
 Ladybugs are beetles. They have wings. They can fly.

They have two sets of wings. One set is hard. It's a shell. One is for flying. They have six legs.

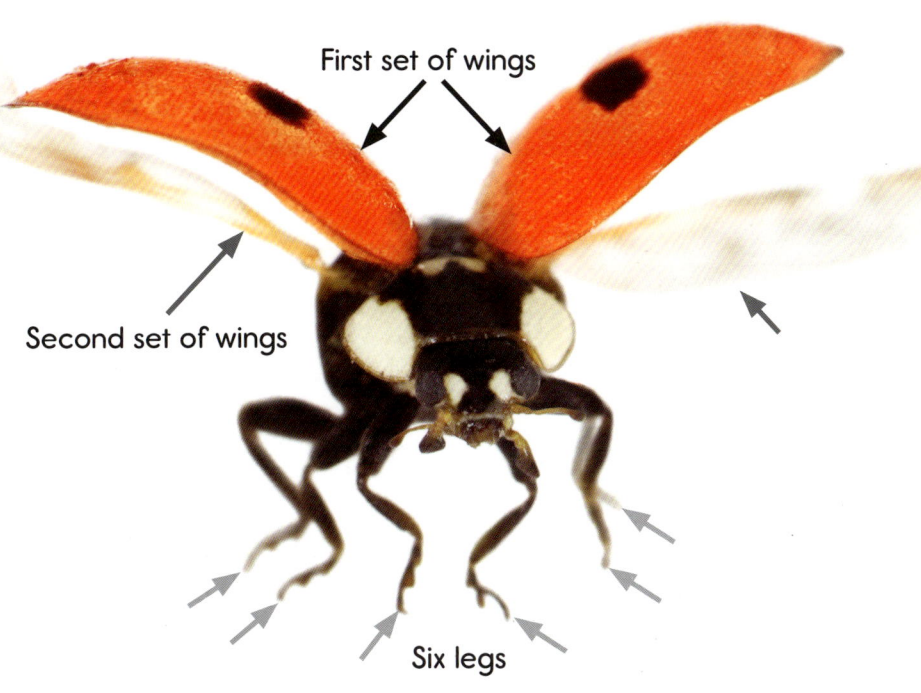

This ladybug just laid eggs.

More Ladybugs

Ladybugs lay their eggs in spring. They lay them on a leaf when it is warm. The eggs will hatch. Soon there will be more ladybugs!

These are eggs laid by a ladybug.

Many bugs don't live long. Ladybugs live up to a year.

Ladybugs eat other insects on farm crops.

Ladybug Helpers

Ladybugs are helpers. They help farmers. They eat <u>pests</u>.

This ladybug is eating <u>aphids</u>.

GLOSSARY

<u>aphids</u>
small bugs that feed by sucking sap from plants

<u>defense</u>
defending from or resisting attack

<u>myths</u>
popular beliefs or traditions that have grown up around something or someone

<u>pests</u>
destructive insects or other animals that attack crops, food, and livestock

<u>poison</u>
a substance that is destructive or harmful